W9-DDW-830

To

_____

From

_____

Date

_____

The quoted ideas expressed in this book (but not Scripture verses) are not, in all cases, exact quotations, as some have been edited for clarity and brevity. In all cases, the author has attempted to maintain the speaker's original intent. In some cases, quoted material for this book was obtained from secondary sources, primarily print media. While every effort was made to ensure the accuracy of these sources, the accuracy cannot be guaranteed. For additions, deletions, corrections, or clarifications in future editions of this text, please write Freeman-Smith, LLC.

Scripture quotations are taken from:

The Holy Bible, King James Version

The Holy Bible, New International Version (NIV) Copyright © 1973, 1978, 1984, by International Bible Society. Used by permission of Zondervan Publishing House. All rights reserved.

The Holy Bible, New King James Version (NKJV) Copyright © 1982 by Thomas Nelson, Inc. Used by permission.

The New American Standard Bible®, (NASB) Copyright © 1960, 1962, 1963, 1968, 1971, 1972, 1973, 1975, 1977, 1995 by The Lockman Foundation. Used by permission.

Holy Bible, New Living Translation, (NLT) Copyright © 1996. Used by permission of Tyndale House Publishers, Inc., Wheaton, Illinois 60189. All rights reserved.

New Century Version®. (NCV) Copyright © 1987, 1988, 1991 by Word Publishing, a division of Thomas Nelson, Inc. All rights reserved. Used by permission.

The Holman Christian Standard Bible™ (Holman CSB) Copyright © 1999, 2000, 2001 by Holman Bible Publishers. Used by permission.

Cover Design by Kim Russell / Wahoo Designs
Page Layout by Bart Dawson

ISBN-13 978-1-58334-397-5

ISBN-10 1-58334-397-0

Printed in the United States of America

Why *Christ* MATTERS...
in your everyday life

Dr. Criswell Freeman

TABLE OF CONTENTS

INTRODUCTION

As you reflect upon your priorities for life, the first question you should ask yourself is whether you believe that this life is the only life you'll ever have. If you believe that life here on earth is a one-way ticket to the grave with no hope of an afterlife, then you will most certainly want to plan your affairs accordingly. But, if you believe that God really does sit in His heaven, and if you believe that His Son Jesus really did die for your sins, then your priorities for this life must include preparations for the next one.

The hymn by Fanny Crosby contains a familiar refrain: "Tell me the story of Jesus." That story, of course, is one that we cannot tell or hear too often. Jesus is the sovereign Friend and ultimate Savior of mankind. Christ showed enduring love for His believers by willingly sacrificing His own life so that we might have eternal life. Now, it is our turn to return His love by inviting Him into our hearts—for Christians, that's Priority #1.

This text contains 30 devotional readings that are intended to remind you of the role that Jesus should play in your everyday life. The ideas on these pages offer Biblically-based, time-tested principles for finding abundance, peace, and joy. So today—and every day—give Christ the respect He deserves. You owe it to Him . . . and to yourself.

Chapter 1

YOUR RELATIONSHIP WITH JESUS

*"I am the bread of life," Jesus told them.
"No one who comes to Me will ever be hungry,
and no one who believes in Me
will ever be thirsty again."*

—

John 6:35 Holman CSB

What is "real" Christianity? Think of it as an ongoing relationship—an all-encompassing relationship with God and with His Son Jesus. It is inevitable that your life must be lived in relationship to God. The question is not if you will have a relationship with Him; the burning question is whether that relationship will be one that seeks to honor Him or one that seeks to ignore Him.

We live in a world that discourages heartfelt devotion and obedience to God. Everywhere we turn, or so it seems, we are confronted by a mind-numbing assortment of distractions, temptations, obligations, and frustrations. Yet even on our busiest days, God beckons us to slow down and consult Him. When we do, we avail ourselves of the peace and abundance that only He can give.

Is Jesus an integral part of your everyday life, or do you relegate Him to a few hours on Sunday mornings? And as you think about the answer to that question, remember that Jesus is always available, and He's waiting to hear from you now. The rest, of course, is up to you.

In the "Grace Plan" God says, "I see the gap and I know you can't make it by your own human strength, so I'm going to send Christ, My Son, to pay for the shortfall. Salvation and adoption into My family will be made available to you as a gift."

Bill Hybels

We shall find in Christ enough of everything we need—for the body, for the mind, and for the spirit—to do what He wants us to do as long as He wants us to do it.

Vance Havner

We must think of the Son always, so to speak, streaming forth from the Father, like light from a lamp, or heat from a fire, or thoughts from a mind. He is the self-expression of the Father— what the Father has to say. And there never was a time when He was not saying it.

C. S. Lewis

To this end was I born, and for this cause came I into the world, that I should bear witness unto the truth.

John 18:37 KJV

For the Son of man is come to save that which was lost.

Matthew 18:11 KJV

Therefore if any man be in Christ, he is a new creature: old things are passed away; behold, all things are become new.

2 Corinthians 5:17 KJV

A PRAYER

Dear Heavenly Father, I praise You and thank You for Your priceless gift: Jesus Christ. Let me share the Good News of the One who became a man so that I might become His, not only for today, but also for all eternity. Jesus is my Savior and my strength. I will welcome Him into my heart with love and thanksgiving, today and forever. Amen

---

Chapter 2

Christ Matters Because…

HE OFFERS THE PRICELESS GIFT OF ETERNAL LIFE

*I have written these things to you
who believe in the name of the Son of God,
so that you may know
that you have eternal life.*

—

1 John 5:13 Holman CSB

Eternal life is not an event that begins when you die. Eternal life begins when you invite Jesus into your heart right here on earth. So it's important to remember that God's plans for you are not limited to the ups and downs of everyday life. If you've allowed Jesus to reign over your heart, you've already begun your eternal journey.

As mere mortals, our vision for the future, like our lives here on earth, is limited. God's vision is not burdened by such limitations: His plans extend throughout all eternity.

Let us praise the Creator for His priceless gift, and let us share the Good News with all who cross our paths. We return our Father's love by accepting His grace and by sharing His message and His love. When we do, we are blessed here on earth and throughout all eternity.

Teach us to set our hopes on heaven, to hold firmly to the promise of eternal life, so that we can withstand the struggles and storms of this world.

Max Lucado

If you are a believer, your judgment will not determine your eternal destiny. Christ's finished work on Calvary was applied to you the moment you accepted Christ as Savior.

Beth Moore

And because we know Christ is alive, we have hope for the present and hope for life beyond the grave.

Billy Graham

The unfolding of our friendship with the Father will be a never-ending revelation stretching on into eternity.

Catherine Marshall

We do not want you to be uninformed, brothers, concerning those who are asleep, so that you will not grieve like the rest, who have no hope. Since we believe that Jesus died and rose again, in the same way God will bring with Him those who have fallen asleep through Jesus.

1 Thessalonians 4:13-14 Holman CSB

Jesus said to her, "I am the resurrection and the life. The one who believes in Me, even if he dies, will live. Everyone who lives and believes in Me will never die—ever. Do you believe this?"

John 11:25-26 Holman CSB

A PRAYER

I know, Lord, that this world is not my home; I am only here for a brief while. And, You have given me the priceless gift of eternal life through Your Son Jesus. Keep the hope of heaven fresh in my heart, and, while I am in this world, help me to pass through it with faith in my heart and praise on my lips . . . for You. Amen

Chapter 3

Christ Matters Because...

HE OFFERS YOU ABUNDANCE

My purpose is to give life in all its fullness.

—

John 10:10 Holman CSB

God offers us abundance through His Son Jesus. Whether or not we accept God's abundance is, of course, up to each of us. When we entrust our hearts and our days to the One who created us, we experience abundance through the grace and sacrifice of His Son Jesus. But, when we turn our thoughts and our energies away from God's commandments, we inevitably forfeit the spiritual abundance that might otherwise be ours.

What is your focus today? Are you focused on God's Word and His will for your life? Or are you focused on the distractions and temptations of a difficult world? The answer to this question will, to a surprising extent, determine the quality and the direction of your day.

If you sincerely seek the spiritual abundance that your Savior offers, then follow Him completely and without reservation. When you do, you will receive the love, the life, and the abundance that He has promised.

Jesus intended for us to be overwhelmed by the blessings of regular days. He said it was the reason he had come: "I am come that they might have life, and that they might have it more abundantly."

Gloria Gaither

Jesus wants Life for us, Life with a capital L.

John Eldredge

People, places, and things were never meant to give us life. God alone is the author of a fulfilling life.

Gary Smalley & John Trent

The only way you can experience abundant life is to surrender your plans to Him.

Charles Stanley

Instead of living a black-and-white existence, we'll be released into a Technicolor world of vibrancy and emotion when we more accurately reflect His nature to the world around us.

Bill Hybels

And God is able to make every grace overflow to you, so that in every way, always having everything you need, you may excel in every good work.

2 Corinthians 9:8 Holman CSB

Until now you have asked for nothing in My name. Ask and you will receive, that your joy may be complete.

John 16:24 Holman CSB

Come to terms with God and be at peace; in this way good will come to you.

Job 22:21 Holman CSB

A PRAYER

Thank You, Lord, for the abundant life given through Your Son Jesus Christ. You have blessed me beyond measure. Use me today and every day to be a blessing to others so that I might share Your abundance with all who cross my path. Amen

Chapter 4

Christ Matters Because...

HE IS WITH YOU DURING DIFFICULT DAYS

I will be with you when you pass through the waters . . . when you walk through the fire . . . the flame will not burn you. For I the Lord your God, the Holy One of Israel, and your Savior.

—

Isaiah 43:2-3 Holman CSB

On occasion, all of us face adversity. Throughout the seasons of life, we must all endure life-altering personal losses that leave us breathless. When we do, God stands ready to protect us. Psalm 147 promises, "He heals the brokenhearted, and binds their wounds" (v. 3 NASB). God keeps His promises. When we are troubled, we can call upon Him, and—in His own time and according to His own plan—He will heal us.

Sometimes, of course, it is not us, but instead our friends, who face adversity. When friends or family members face troubling times, our mission is simple: We must assist in any way we can, either with an encouraging word, a helping hand, or a heartfelt prayer.

The English clergyman Charles Kingsley had practical advice for Christian friends of every generation. He advised, "Make it a rule, and pray to God to help you to keep it, never, if possible, to lie down at night without being able to say: 'I have made one human being at least a little wiser, or a little happier, or at least a little better this day.'" Amen to that . . . especially in times of adversity.

We must face today as children of tomorrow. We must meet the uncertainties of this world with the certainty of the world to come. To the pure in heart nothing really bad can happen . . . not death, but sin, should be our greatest fear.

A. W. Tozer

A faith that hasn't been tested can't be trusted.

Adrian Rogers

Often, in the midst of great problems, we stop short of the real blessing God has for us, which is a fresh vision of who He is.

Anne Graham Lotz

God will never let you sink under your circumstances. He always provides a safety net and His love always encircles.

Barbara Johnson

Our loving God uses difficulty in our lives to burn away the sin of self and build faith and spiritual power.

Bill Bright

When you are in distress and all these things have happened to you, you will return to the Lord your God in later days and obey Him. He will not leave you, destroy you, or forget the covenant with your fathers that He swore to them by oath, because the Lord your God is a compassionate God.

Deuteronomy 4:30-31 Holman CSB

Dear friends, when the fiery ordeal arises among you to test you, don't be surprised by it, as if something unusual were happening to you. Instead, as you share in the sufferings of the Messiah rejoice, so that you may also rejoice with great joy at the revelation of His glory.

1 Peter 4:12-13 Holman CSB

A PRAYER

Heavenly Father, You are my strength and refuge. I can face the difficulties of this day because You are with me. You are my light and pathway. As I follow You, Father, I can overcome adversity just as Jesus overcame this world. Amen

Chapter 5

Christ Matters Because...

HE OFFERS HOPE

For the grace of God that brings salvation has appeared to all men, teaching us that, denying ungodliness and worldly lusts, we should live soberly, righteously, and godly in the present age, looking for the blessed hope and glorious appearing of our great God and Savior Jesus Christ.

—

Titus 2:11-13 NKJV

Look around you. Read the newspaper. Watch the evening news. When you think about the things that are going on in Washington or elsewhere in the world, it's possible to lose hope. But God provides an antidote to despair. One of the rewards of spending time before the face of God is the gift of divine hope.

Have you ever felt your hope in the future slipping away? If so, here's what you should do: study God's Word, seek God's will, and spend prayerful hours before God's face. When you do, you'll discover the hope that is the possession of those who place their trust in Him.

This world can be a place of trials and tribulations, but as believers in Christ we are secure. We need never lose hope because God has promised us peace, joy, and eternal life. So, let us face each day with hope in our hearts and trust in our God. And, let us teach our children to do likewise. After all, God has promised us that we are His throughout eternity, and He keeps His promises. Always.

I wish I could make it all new again; I can't.
But God can. "He restores my soul," wrote the
shepherd. God doesn't reform; he restores. He
doesn't camouflage the old; he restores the new.
The Master Builder will pull out the original
plan and restore it.

Max Lucado

Faith looks back and draws courage; hope looks
ahead and keeps desire alive.

John Eldredge

I discovered that sorrow was not to be feared but
rather endured with hope and expectancy that
God would use it to visit and bless my life.

Jill Briscoe

Hope is nothing more than the expectation of
those things which faith has believed to be truly
promised by God.

John Calvin

Let us hold on to the confession of our hope without wavering, for He who promised is faithful.

Hebrews 10:23 Holman CSB

Hope deferred makes the heart sick.

Proverbs 13:12 NKJV

Sustain me as You promised, and I will live; do not let me be ashamed of my hope.

Psalm 119:116 Holman CSB

A PRAYER

Dear Lord, make me a hope-filled Christian. If I become discouraged, let me turn to You. If I grow weary, let me seek strength in You. In every aspect of my life, I will trust You, Father, today and forever. Amen

Chapter 6

Christ Matters Because...

WHEN YOU FOLLOW HIM, YOU WILL BE BLESSED

But whoever keeps His word, truly in him the love of God is perfected. This is how we know we are in Him: the one who says he remains in Him should walk just as He walked.

—

1 John 2:5-6 Holman CSB

Jesus walks with you. Are you walking with Him? Hopefully, you will choose to walk with Him today and every day of your life.

Jesus loved you so much that He endured unspeakable humiliation and suffering for you. How will you respond to Christ's sacrifice? Will you take up His cross and follow Him (Luke 9:23), or will you choose another path? When you place your hopes squarely at the foot of the cross, when you place Jesus squarely at the center of your life, you will be blessed.

The old familiar hymn begins, "What a friend we have in Jesus . . . ." No truer words were ever penned. Jesus is the sovereign Friend and ultimate Savior of mankind. Christ showed enduring love for His believers by willingly sacrificing His own life so that we might have eternal life. Now, it is our turn to become His friend.

Let us love our Savior, let us praise Him, and let us share His message of salvation with the world. When we do, we demonstrate that our acquaintance with the Master is not a passing fancy, but is, instead, the cornerstone and the touchstone of our lives.

Our responsibility is to feed from Him, to stay close to Him, to follow Him—because sheep easily go astray—so that we eternally experience the protection and companionship of our Great Shepherd the Lord Jesus Christ.

Franklin Graham

Living life with a consistent spiritual walk deeply influences those we love most.

Vonette Bright

A believer comes to Christ; a disciple follows after Him.

Vance Havner

You cannot cooperate with Jesus in becoming what He wants you to become and simultaneously be what the world desires to make you. If you would say, "Take the world but give me Jesus," then you must deny yourself and take up your cross. The simple truth is that your "self" must be put to death in order for you to get to the point where for you to live is Christ. What will it be? The world and you, or Jesus and you? You do have a choice to make.

Kay Arthur

We encouraged, comforted, and implored each one of you to walk worthy of God, who calls you into His own kingdom and glory.

1 Thessalonians 2:12 Holman CSB

The one who loves his life will lose it, and the one who hates his life in this world will keep it for eternal life. If anyone serves Me, he must follow Me. Where I am, there My servant also will be. If anyone serves Me, the Father will honor him.

John 12:25-26 Holman CSB

Follow Me, Jesus told them, "and I will make you into fishers of men!" Immediately they left their nets and followed Him.

Mark 1:17-18 Holman CSB

A PRAYER

Dear Jesus, because I am Your disciple, I will trust You, I will obey Your teachings, and I will share Your Good News. You have given me life abundant and life eternal, and I will follow You today and forever. Amen

Christ Matters Because...
HE IS THE
GREAT HEALER

*And the power of the Lord
was present to heal them.*

—

Luke 5:17 NKJV

Jesus overcame the world, and He promised that we can overcome it, too. But sometimes, we really don't feel strong enough to overcome anything. Sometimes we experience life-changing personal losses that leave us feeling downhearted, discouraged, or worse. When we do, we should remember Christ's assurances, and we should remember that God stands ready to protect us. When we are deeply troubled, we must call upon God, and then, in His own time and according to His own plan, He will heal us.

Are you anxious? Take those anxieties to God. Are you troubled? Take your troubles to Him. Does your world seem to be trembling beneath your feet? Seek protection from the One who cannot be moved. The same God who created the universe will protect you if you ask Him . . . so ask Him.

Ultimate healing and the glorification of the body are certainly among the blessings of Calvary for the believing Christian. Immediate healing is not guaranteed.

Warren Wiersbe

Jesus Christ is the One by Whom, for Whom, through Whom everything was made. Therefore, He knows what's wrong in your life and how to fix it.

Anne Graham Lotz

People are funny. When they are young, they will spend their health to get wealth. Later, they will gladly pay all they have trying to get their health back.

John Maxwell

You can't buy good health at the doctor's office—you've got to earn it for yourself.

Marie T. Freeman

I have heard your prayer; I have seen your tears. Look, I will heal you.

2 Kings 20:5 Holman CSB

Peter said to him, "Aeneas, Jesus Christ heals you. Get up and make your own bed," and immediately he got up.

Acts 9:34 Holman CSB

For I am the Lord who heals you.

Exodus 15:26 Holman CSB

A PRAYER

Dear Lord, place Your healing hand upon me. Heal my body and my soul. Let me trust Your promises, Father, and let me turn to You for hope, for restoration, for renewal, and for salvation. Amen

Chapter 8

Christ Matters Because...

HE IS WITH YOU ALWAYS

*Lo, I am with you always,
even unto the end of the world.*

—

Matthew 28:20 KJV

Do you ever wonder if God is really here? If so, you're not the first person to think such thoughts. In fact, some of the biggest heroes in the Bible had their doubts—and so, perhaps, will you. But when questions arise and doubts begin to creep into your mind, remember this: God hasn't gone on vacation; He hasn't left town; and He doesn't have an unlisted number. You can talk with Him any time you feel like it. In fact, He's right here, right now, listening to your thoughts and prayers, watching over your every move.

Sometimes, you will allow yourself to become very busy, and that's when you may be tempted to ignore God. But, when you quiet yourself long enough to acknowledge His presence, God will touch your heart and restore your spirits. By the way, He's ready to talk right now. Are you?

The world, space, and all visible components reverberate with God's Presence and demonstrate His Mighty Power.

Franklin Graham

It is God to whom and with whom we travel, while He is the End of our journey, He is also at every stopping place.

Elisabeth Elliot

God expresses His love toward us by His uninterrupted presence in our lives.

Charles Stanley

We are never more fulfilled than when our longing for God is met by His presence in our lives.

Billy Graham

Give yourself a gift today: be present with yourself. God is. Enjoy your own personality. God does.

Barbara Johnson

Draw near to God, and He will draw near to you.

James 4:8 Holman CSB

You will seek Me and find Me when you search for Me with all your heart.

Jeremiah 29:13 Holman CSB

The Lord is near all who call out to Him, all who call out to Him with integrity. He fulfills the desires of those who fear Him; He hears their cry for help and saves them.

Psalm 145:18-19 Holman CSB

A PRAYER

Dear Lord, You are with me always. Help me feel Your presence in every situation and every circumstance. Today, Dear God, let me feel You and acknowledge Your presence, Your love, and Your Son. Amen

Chapter 9

Christ Matters Because...

HE GIVES YOU
THE STRENGTH
TO PERSEVERE

*Let us run with endurance the race that is set
before us, looking unto Jesus, the author and
finisher of our faith, who for the joy that was set
before Him endured the cross, despising
the shame, and has sat down at the right hand
of the throne of God.*

—

Hebrews 12:1-2 NKJV

A well-lived life is like a marathon, not a sprint—it calls for preparation, determination, and, of course, lots of perseverance. As an example of perfect perseverance, we Christians need look no further than our Savior, Jesus Christ.

Jesus finished what He began. Despite His suffering and despite the shame of the cross, Jesus was steadfast in His faithfulness to God. We, too, must remain faithful, especially during times of hardship. Sometimes, God may answer our prayers with silence, and when He does, we must patiently persevere.

Are you facing a tough situation? If so, remember this: whatever your problem, God can handle it. Your job is to keep persevering until He does.

Failure is one of life's most powerful teachers.
How we handle our failures determines whether
we're going to simply "get by" in life or "press on."

Beth Moore

When you persevere through a trial, God gives
you a special measure of insight.

Charles Swindoll

Jesus taught that perseverance is the essential
element in prayer.

E. M. Bounds

I learned as never before that persistent calling
upon the Lord breaks through every stronghold
of the devil, for nothing is impossible with God.
For Christians in these troubled times, there is
simply no other way.

Jim Cymbala

Do you not know that the runners in a stadium all race, but only one receives the prize? Run in such a way that you may win. Now everyone who competes exercises self-control in everything. However, they do it to receive a perishable crown, but we an imperishable one.

1 Corinthians 9:24-25 Holman CSB

But as for you, be strong; don't be discouraged, for your work has a reward.

2 Chronicles 15:7 Holman CSB

A PRAYER

Dear Lord, life is not a sprint, but a marathon. When the pace of my life becomes frantic, slow me down and give me perspective. Keep me steady and sure. When I become weary, let me persevere so that, in Your time, I might finish my work here on earth, and that You might then say, "Well done my good and faithful servant." Amen

Chapter 10

Christ Matters Because...

HE WILL GUIDE YOUR THOUGHTS TO THINGS ABOVE

*If then you were raised with Christ,
seek those things which are above,
where Christ is, sitting at the right hand of God.
Set your mind on things above,
not on things on the earth.*

—

Colossians 3:1-2 NKJV

When you decided to allow Christ to rule over your heart, you entitled yourself to share in His promise of spiritual abundance and eternal joy. Have you claimed that entitlement? Are you an upbeat believer? Are you a person whose hopes and dreams are alive and well? Hopefully so. But sometimes, when pessimism and doubt invade your thoughts, you won't feel like celebrating. Why? Because thoughts are extremely powerful things.

If you've allowed pessimism to creep into your mind and heart, you should spend more time thinking about your blessings and less time fretting about your hardships. Then, you should take time to thank the Giver of all things good for gifts that are, in truth, far too numerous to count.

No more imperfect thoughts. No more sad memories. No more ignorance. My redeemed body will have a redeemed mind. Grant me a foretaste of that perfect mind as you mirror your thoughts in me today.

Joni Eareckson Tada

People who do not develop and practice good thinking often find themselves at the mercy of their circumstances.

John Maxwell

It is the thoughts and intents of the heart that shape a person's life.

John Eldredge

Your thoughts are the determining factor as to whose mold you are conformed to. Control your thoughts and you control the direction of your life.

Charles Stanley

Attitude is the mind's paintbrush; it can color any situation.

Barbara Johnson

As for you, Solomon my son, know the God of your father, and serve Him with a whole heart and a willing mind, for the Lord searches every heart and understands the intention of every thought. If you seek Him, He will be found by you, but if you forsake Him, He will reject you forever.

1 Chronicles 28:9 Holman CSB

I, the Lord, examine the mind, I test the heart to give to each according to his way, according to what his actions deserve.

Jeremiah 17:10 Holman CSB

A PRAYER

Dear Lord, keep my thoughts focused on Your love, Your power, Your promises, and Your Son. When I am worried, I will turn to You for comfort; when I am weak, I will turn to You for strength; when I am troubled, I will turn to You for patience and perspective. Help me guard my thoughts, Father, so that I may honor You today and every day that I live. Amen

Chapter 11

Christ Matters Because...

HE IS THE PERFECT EXAMPLE

*For I have given you an example
that you also should do
just as I have done for you.*

—

John 13:15 Holman CSB

Whether we like it or not, all of us are role models. Our friends and family members watch our actions and, as followers of Christ, we are obliged to act accordingly.

What kind of example are you? Are you the kind of person whose life serves as a genuine example of righteousness? Are you the kind of person whose behavior serves as a positive role model for others? Are you the kind of person whose actions, day in and day out, are based upon kindness, faithfulness, and a love for the Lord? If so, you are not only blessed by God, but you are also a powerful force for good in a world that desperately needs positive influences such as yours.

We live in a dangerous, temptation-filled world. That's why you encounter so many opportunities to stray from God's commandments. Resist those temptations! When you do, you'll earn God's blessings and you'll serve as a positive role model for your family and friends.

Corrie ten Boom advised, "Don't worry about what you do not understand. Worry about what you do understand in the Bible but do not live by." And that's sound advice because our families and friends are watching . . . and so, for that matter, is God.

You can never separate a leader's actions from his character.

John Maxwell

The sermon of your life in tough times ministers to people more powerfully than the most eloquent speaker.

Bill Bright

What we practice, not (save at rare intervals) what we preach, is usually our great contribution to the conversion of others.

C. S. Lewis

Our walk counts far more than our talk, always!

George Mueller

You should be an example to the believers in speech, in conduct, in love, in faith, in purity.

1 Timothy 4:12 Holman CSB

Do everything without grumbling and arguing, so that you may be blameless and pure.

Philippians 2:14–15 Holman CSB

Set an example of good works yourself, with integrity and dignity in your teaching.

Titus 2:7 Holman CSB

A PRAYER

Lord, make me a worthy example to my family and friends. And, let my words and my deeds serve as a testimony to the changes You have made in my life. Let me praise You, Father, by following in the footsteps of Your Son, and let others see Him through me. Amen

Chapter 12

Christ Matters Because...

HE GIVES YOU COMFORT IN TIMES OF SORROW

*Blessed are those who mourn,
because they will be comforted.*

—

Matthew 5:4 Holman CSB

Grief visits all of us who live long and love deeply. When we lose a loved one, or when we experience any other profound loss, darkness overwhelms us for a while, and it seems as if our purpose for living has vanished. Thankfully, God has other plans.

The Christian faith, as communicated through the words of the Holy Bible, is a healing faith. It offers comfort in times of trouble, courage for our fears, hope instead of hopelessness. For Christians, the grave is not a final resting-place, it is a place of transition. Through the healing words of God's promises, Christians understand that the Lord continues to manifest His plan in good times and bad.

If you are experiencing the intense pain of a recent loss, or if you are still mourning a loss from long ago, perhaps you are now ready to begin the next stage of your journey with God. If so, be mindful of this fact: As a wounded survivor, you will have countless opportunities to serve others. And by serving others, you will bring purpose and meaning to the suffering you've endured.

I discovered that sorrow was not to be feared but rather endured with hope and expectancy that God would use it to visit and bless my life.

Jill Briscoe

You learn your theology most where your sorrows take you.

Martin Luther

Many of God's plants grow best in the dark, and he often puts them in the dark to make them grow.

C. H. Spurgeon

Our times of trouble, heartache, and sorrow can be God's holy love refinery that makes us the kind of people that He wants us to be.

Bill Bright

I have heard your prayer; I have seen your tears. Look, I will heal you.

2 Kings 20:5 Holman CSB

Blessed are you who are hungry now, because you will be filled. Blessed are you who weep now, because you will laugh.

Luke 6:21 Holman CSB

I called to the Lord in my distress; I called to my God. From His temple He heard my voice.

2 Samuel 22:7 Holman CSB

A PRAYER

You have promised, Lord, that You will not give me any more than I can bear. You have promised to lift me out of my grief and despair. You have promised to put a new song on my lips. I thank You, Lord, for sustaining me in my day of sorrow. Restore me, and heal me, and use me as You will. Amen

Chapter 13

Christ Matters Because...

HE OFFERS
REAL LIFE

*Anyone finding his life will lose it,
and anyone losing his life because
of Me will find it.*

—

Matthew 10:39 Holman CSB

Life is God's gift to you, and He intends that you celebrate His glorious gift. If you're a person who treasures each day—and if you teach others to do the same—you will be blessed by your Father in heaven.

For Christians, every day begins and ends with God and His Son. Christ came to this earth to give us abundant life and eternal salvation. Our task is to accept Christ's grace with joy in our hearts and praise on our lips. Believers who fashion their days around Jesus are transformed: They see the world differently, they act differently, and they feel differently about themselves and their neighbors.

Christian believers face the inevitable challenges and disappointments of each day armed with the joy of Christ and the promise of salvation. So whatever this day holds for you, begin it and end it with God as your partner and Christ as your Savior. And throughout the day, give thanks to the One who created you and saved you. God's love for you is infinite. Accept it joyously and be thankful.

Like a shadow declining swiftly . . . away . . .
like the dew of the morning gone with the heat
of the day; like the wind in the treetops, like a
wave of the sea, so are our lives on earth when
seen in light of eternity.

Ruth Bell Graham

The value of a life can only be estimated by its
relationship to God.

Oswald Chambers

The world has never been stable. Jesus Himself
was born into the cruelest and most unstable of
worlds. No, we have babies and keep trusting
and living because the Resurrection is true! The
Resurrection was not just a one-time event in
history; it is a principle built into the very fabric
of our beings, a fact reverberating from every
cell of creation: Life wins! Life wins!

Gloria Gaither

A life lived without reflection can be very
superficial and empty.

Elisabeth Elliot

I am the Alpha and the Omega, the Beginning and the End. I will give to the thirsty from the spring of living water as a gift.

Revelation 21:6 Holman CSB

Teach us to number our days carefully so that we may develop wisdom in our hearts.

Psalm 90:12 Holman CSB

For to me to live is Christ, and to die is gain.

Philippians 1:21 KJV

A PRAYER

Lord, You are the Giver of all life, and You created me to have fellowship with You. Let me live a life that pleases You, Lord, and let me thank You always for Your blessings. You love me and protect me, Heavenly Father. Let me be grateful, and let me live for You today and throughout eternity. Amen

Chapter 14

Christ Matters Because...

HE IS SUFFICIENT TO MEET YOUR NEEDS

*For His divine power has given us everything
required for life and godliness,
through the knowledge of Him who called us
by His own glory and goodness.*

—

2 Peter 1:3 Holman CSB

It is easy to become overwhelmed by the demands of everyday life, but if you're a faithful follower of the One from Galilee, you need never be overwhelmed. Why? Because God's love is sufficient to meet your needs. Whatever dangers you may face, whatever heartbreaks you must endure, God is with you, and He stands ready to comfort you and to heal you.

The Psalmist writes, "Weeping may endure for a night, but joy comes in the morning" (Psalm 30:5 NKJV). But when we are suffering, the morning may seem very far away. It is not. God promises that He is "near to those who have a broken heart" (Psalm 34:18 NKJV).

If you are experiencing the intense pain of a recent loss, or if you are still mourning a loss from long ago, perhaps you are now ready to begin the next stage of your journey with God. If so, be mindful of this fact: the loving heart of God is sufficient to meet any challenge, including yours.

God's all-sufficiency is a major. Your inability is a minor. Major in majors, not in minors.

Corrie ten Boom

Let your faith in Christ be in the quiet confidence that He will, every day and every moment, keep you as the apple of His eye, keep you in perfect peace and in the sure experience of all the light and the strength you need.

Andrew Murray

God has a course mapped out for your life, and all the inadequacies in the world will not change His mind. He will be with you every step of the way. And though it may take time, He has a celebration planned for when you cross over the "Red Seas" of your life.

Charles Swindoll

The Lord is the one who travels every mile of the wilderness way as our leader, cheering us, supporting and supplying and fortifying us.

Elisabeth Elliot

The LORD is my strength and song, and He has become my salvation; He is my God, and I will praise Him . . . .

Exodus 15:2 NKJV

Peace, peace to you, and peace to your helpers! For your God helps you.

1 Chronicles 12:18 NKJV

He gives power to the weak, and to those who have no might He increases strength.

Isaiah 40:29 NKJV

A PRAYER

Dear Lord, whatever "it" is, You can handle it! Let me turn to You when I am fearful or worried. You are my loving Heavenly Father, sufficient in all things and I will always trust You. Amen

Chapter 15

Christ Matters Because...

HE CALMS
YOUR HEART

*Be anxious for nothing, but in everything
by prayer and supplication, with thanksgiving,
let your requests be made known to God.*

—

Philippians 4:6 NKJV

We live in a world that often breeds anxiety and fear. When we come face to face with tough times, we may fall prey to discouragement, doubt, or depression. But our Father in heaven has other plans. God has promised that we may lead lives of abundance, not anxiety. In fact, His Word instructs us to "be anxious for nothing." But how can we put our fears to rest? By taking those fears to God and leaving them there.

As you face the challenges of everyday living, do you find yourself becoming anxious, troubled, discouraged, or fearful? If so, turn every one of your concerns over to your Heavenly Father. The same God who created the universe will comfort you if you ask Him . . . so ask Him and trust Him. And then watch in amazement as your anxieties melt into the warmth of His loving hands.

When you are anxious, it means that you aren't trusting God completely; it means that you aren't trusting God to take care of your needs.

Stormie Omartian

The thing that preserves a man from panic is his relationship to God.

Oswald Chambers

Anxiety may be natural and normal for the world, but it is not to be part of a believer's lifestyle.

Kay Arthur

The beginning of anxiety is the end of faith, and the beginning of true faith is the end of anxiety.

George Mueller

Much that worries us beforehand can, quite unexpectedly, have a happy and simple solution. Worries just don't matter. Things really are in a better hand than ours.

Dietrich Bonhoeffer

Therefore don't worry about tomorrow, because tomorrow will worry about itself. Each day has enough trouble of its own.

Matthew 6:34 Holman CSB

Anxiety in a man's heart weighs it down, but a good word cheers it up.

Proverbs 12:25 Holman CSB

Why am I so depressed? Why this turmoil within me? Put your hope in God, for I will still praise Him, my Savior and my God.

Psalm 42:11 Holman CSB

A PRAYER

Lord, when I am tempted to lose faith in the future, touch my heart with Your enduring love. And, keep me mindful, Lord, that nothing, absolutely nothing, will happen this day that You and I cannot handle together. Amen

Chapter 16

Christ Matters Because...
HE GIVES YOU COURAGE

Immediately Jesus spoke to them.
"Have courage! It is I. Don't be afraid."

Matthew 14:27 Holman CSB

Christians have every reason to live courageously. After all, the ultimate battle has already been fought and won on the cross at Calvary. But, even dedicated followers of Christ may find their courage tested by the inevitable disappointments and tragedies that occur in the lives of believers and non-believers alike.

Every human life is a tapestry of events: some wonderful, some not-so-wonderful, and some downright disheartening. When the storm clouds form overhead and we find ourselves wandering through the dark valley of despair, our faith is stretched, sometimes to the breaking point. But as believers, we can be comforted: Wherever we find ourselves, whether at the top of the mountain or the depths of the valley, God is there, and because He cares for us, we can live courageously.

The next time you find yourself in a fear-provoking situation, remember that God is as near as your next breath, and remember that He offers salvation to His children. He is your shield and your strength; He is your protector and your deliverer. Call upon Him in your hour of need and then be comforted. Whatever your challenge, whatever your trouble, God can handle it. And will.

Take courage. We walk in the wilderness today and in the Promised Land tomorrow.

D. L. Moody

When once we are assured that God is good, then there can be nothing left to fear.

Hannah Whitall Smith

There comes a time when we simply have to face the challenges in our lives and stop backing down.

John Eldredge

Why rely on yourself and fall? Cast yourself upon His arm. Be not afraid. He will not let you slip. Cast yourself in confidence. He will receive you and heal you.

St. Augustine

Be strong and courageous, and do the work. Don't be afraid or discouraged, for the Lord God, my God, is with you. He won't leave you or forsake you.

1 Chronicles 28:20 Holman CSB

For God has not given us a spirit of fearfulness, but one of power, love, and sound judgment.

2 Timothy 1:7 Holman CSB

Be alert, stand firm in the faith, be brave and strong.

1 Corinthians 16:13 Holman CSB

A PRAYER

Lord, let me turn to You for courage and for strength. When I am fearful, keep me mindful of Your promises. When I am anxious, let me turn my thoughts and prayers to the priceless gift of Your Son. You are with me always, Heavenly Father, and I will face the challenges of this day with trust and assurance in You. Amen

Chapter 17

Christ Matters Because...

HE OFFERS COMFORT

Blessed be the God and Father of our Lord Jesus Christ, the Father of mercies and the God of all comfort. He comforts us in all our affliction, so that we may be able to comfort those who are in any kind of affliction, through the comfort we ourselves receive from God.

—

2 Corinthians 1:3-4 Holman CSB

We live in a world that is, on occasion, a frightening place. Sometimes, we sustain life-changing losses that are so profound and so tragic that it seems we could never recover. But, with God's help and with the help of encouraging family members and friends, we can recover.

In times of need, friends comfort friends. Our task, as Christians, is to comfort our families and friends by sharing not only our own courage but also the peace and assurance of our Lord and Savior, Christ Jesus. As the renowned revivalist Vance Havner observed, "No journey is complete that does not lead through some dark valleys. We can properly comfort others only with the comfort wherewith we ourselves have been comforted of God."

In times of adversity, we are wise to remember the words of Jesus, who, when He walked on the waters, reassured His disciples, saying, "Take courage! It is I. Don't be afraid" (Matthew 14:27 NIV). Then, with Christ on His throne and trusted friends at our side, we can face our fears with courage and faith.

God's promises are medicine for the broken heart. Let Him comfort you. And, after He has comforted you, try to share that comfort with somebody else. It will do both of you good.

Warren Wiersbe

In Jesus, the service of God and the service of the least of the brethren were one.

Dietrich Bonhoeffer

Discouraged people don't need critics. They hurt enough already. They don't need more guilt or piled-on distress. They need encouragement. They need a refuge, a willing, caring, available someone.

Charles Swindoll

What a comfort to know that God is present there in your life, available to meet every situation with you, that you are never left to face any problem alone.

Vonette Bright

Finally, all of you be of one mind, having compassion for one another; love as brothers, be tenderhearted, be courteous.

1 Peter 3:8 NKJV

Love is patient; love is kind.

1 Corinthians 13:4 Holman CSB

And may the Lord make you increase and abound in love to one another and to all.

1 Thessalonians 3:12 NKJV

A PRAYER

Heavenly Father, sometimes this world can be a difficult place indeed. Let me be a beacon of encouragement to those who have lost hope. Let me comfort those who grieve. And let me share Your love and spread Your Word to a world that needs both. Amen

Chapter 18

Christ Matters Because...
HE CAN HELP
YOU FORGIVE

Then Peter came to Him and said,
"Lord, how many times could my brother sin
against me and I forgive him?
As many as seven times?"
"I tell you, not as many as seven,"
Jesus said to him, "but 70 times seven."

—

Matthew 18:21-22 Holman CSB

Even the most loyal Christian friends may
be quick to judge and slow to forgive. We
human beings, imperfect as we are, seem all
too quick to judge the actions and motivations
of others. The temptation to judge is both
powerful and subtle, but as Christians, we are
commanded to refrain from such behavior. The
warning of Matthew 7:1 is clear: "Judge not,
that ye be not judged." But, as fallible, imperfect
human beings living in a stressful world, we are
sorely tempted to do otherwise.

As Jesus came upon a young woman who
had been condemned by the Pharisees, He spoke
not only to the crowd that was gathered there,
but also to all generations when He warned, "He
that is without sin among you, let him first cast
a stone at her" (John 8:7 KJV). Christ's message
is clear, and it applies not only to the Pharisees
of ancient times, but also to us.

We have all fallen short of God's
commandments, and none of us, therefore, are
qualified to "cast the first stone." Thankfully,
God has forgiven us. We, too, must forgive
others. When we do, we not only obey the
commandment of our Creator, we also free

ourselves from the chains of bitterness and regret.

Only the truly forgiven are truly forgiving.

C. S. Lewis

Jesus had a forgiving and understanding heart. If he lives within us, mercy will temper our relationships with our fellow men.

Billy Graham

Revenge is the raging fire that consumes the arsonist.

Max Lucado

To hold on to hate and resentments is to throw a monkey wrench into the machinery of life.

E. Stanley Jones

*All bitterness, anger and wrath, insult and
slander must be removed from you, along with all
wickedness. And be kind and compassionate to one
another, forgiving one another, just as God also
forgave you in Christ.*

Ephesians 4:31-32 Holman CSB

*See to it that no one repays evil for evil to anyone,
but always pursue what is good for one another and
for all.*

1 Thessalonians 5:15 Holman CSB

*A person's insight gives him patience, and his virtue
is to overlook an offense.*

Proverbs 19:11 Holman CSB

A PRAYER

Dear Lord, sometimes forgiveness is difficult
indeed. Today, Father, I ask You to help me
move beyond feelings of bitterness and anger.
Jesus forgave those who hurt Him; let me walk
in His footsteps by forgiving those who have
injured me. Amen

Chapter 19

Christ Matters Because . . .

HE GAVE HIS LIFE ON THE CROSS FOR YOU

*For Christ did not send me to baptize,
but to preach the gospel—not with clever words,
so that the cross of Christ will not
be emptied of its effect.*

1 Corinthians 1:17 Holman CSB

As we consider Christ's sacrifice on the cross, we should be profoundly humbled and profoundly grateful. And today, as we come to Christ in prayer, we should do so in a spirit of quiet, heartfelt devotion to the One who gave His life so that we might have life eternal.

He was the Son of God, but He wore a crown of thorns. He was the Savior of mankind, yet He was put to death on a rough-hewn cross made of wood. He offered His healing touch to an unsaved world, and yet the same hands that had healed the sick and raised the dead were pierced with nails.

Christ humbled Himself on a cross—for you. He shed His blood—for you. He has offered to walk with you through this life and throughout all eternity. As you approach Him today in prayer, think about His sacrifice and His grace. And be humble.

Through the death and broken body of Jesus Christ on the Cross, you and I have been given access to the presence of God when we approach Him by faith in prayer.

Anne Graham Lotz

It is because of God's loving grace that Jesus died on the cross for our sins so we could experience an eternal relationship with Him.

Bill Bright

Our confidence in prayer comes not from who we are but from who He is. Nothing we could ask of Him could ever compare with the price He paid for us at the cross.

Henry Blackaby

The cross takes care of the past. The cross takes care of the flesh. The cross takes care of the world.

Kay Arthur

There is no detour to holiness. Jesus came to the resurrection through the cross, not around it.

Leighton Ford

Though He was delivered up according to God's determined plan and foreknowledge, you used lawless people to nail Him to a cross and kill Him. God raised Him up, ending the pains of death, because it was not possible for Him to be held by it.

Acts 2:23-24 Holman CSB

Therefore, my brothers, you also were put to death in relation to the law through the crucified body of the Messiah, so that you may belong to another—to Him who was raised from the dead—that we may bear fruit for God.

Romans 7:4 Holman CSB

A PRAYER

Dear Jesus, You are my Savior and my Protector. You suffered on the cross for me, and I will give You honor and praise every day of my life. I will honor You with my words, my thoughts, and my prayers. And I will live according to Your commandments, so that through me, others might come to know Your perfect love. Amen

Chapter 20

Christ Matters Because...

HE LOVES YOU

Who can separate us from the love of Christ?
Can affliction or anguish or persecution
or famine or nakedness or danger or sword?
. . . No, in all these things we are more than
victorious through Him who loved us.

Romans 8:35, 37 Holman CSB

How much does Christ love us? More than we, as mere mortals, can comprehend. His love is perfect and steadfast. Even though we are fallible and wayward, the Good Shepherd cares for us still. Even though we have fallen far short of the Father's commandments, Christ loves us with a power and depth that are beyond our understanding. The sacrifice that Jesus made upon the cross was made for each of us, and His love endures to the edge of eternity and beyond.

Christ's love changes everything. When you accept His gift of grace, you are transformed, not only for today, but also for all eternity. If you haven't already done so, accept Jesus Christ as your Savior. He's waiting patiently for you to invite Him into your heart. Please don't make Him wait a single minute longer.

It has been the faith of the Son of God who loves me and gave Himself for me that has held me in the darkest valley and the hottest fires and the deepest waters.

Elisabeth Elliot

Live your lives in love, the same sort of love which Christ gives us, and which He perfectly expressed when He gave Himself as a sacrifice to God.

Corrie ten Boom

He loved us not because we're lovable, but because He is love.

C. S. Lewis

If you come to Christ, you will always have the option of an ever-present friend. You don't have to dial long-distance. He'll be with you every step of the way.

Bill Hybels

I am the good shepherd. The good shepherd lays down his life for the sheep.

John 10:11 Holman CSB

But God proves His own love for us in that while we were still sinners Christ died for us!

Romans 5:8 Holman CSB

No one has greater love than this, that someone would lay down his life for his friends.

John 15:13 Holman CSB

A PRAYER

Thank You, Lord, for Your Son. His love is boundless, infinite, and eternal. Today, let me pause and reflect upon Christ's love for me, and let me share that love with all those who cross my path. And, as an expression of my love for Him, let me share Christ's saving message with a world that desperately needs His grace. Amen

Chapter 21

Christ Matters Because...

WHEN YOU OBEY HIM YOU ARE BLESSED

Keep asking, and it will be given to you. Keep searching, and you will find. Keep knocking, and the door will be opened to you.
For everyone who asks receives, and the one who searches finds, and to the one who knocks, the door will be opened.

Matthew 7:7-8 Holman CSB

How can we demonstrate our love for God? By accepting His Son as our personal Savior and by placing Christ squarely at the center of our lives and our hearts. Jesus said that if we are to love Him, we must obey His commandments (John 14:15). Thus, our obedience to the Master is an expression of our love for Him.

In Ephesians 2:10 we read, "For we are His workmanship, created in Christ Jesus for good works" (NKJV). These words are instructive: We are not saved by good works, but for good works. Good works are not the root, but rather the fruit of our salvation.

Today, let the fruits of your stewardship be a clear demonstration of your love for Christ. When you do, your good heart will bring forth many good things for yourself and for God. Christ has given you spiritual abundance and eternal life. You, in turn, owe Him good treasure from a single obedient heart . . . yours.

You may not always see immediate results, but all God wants is your obedience and faithfulness.

Vonette Bright

Trials and sufferings teach us to obey the Lord by faith, and we soon learn that obedience pays off in joyful ways.

Bill Bright

God uses broken things: broken soil and broken clouds to produce grain; broken grain to produce bread; broken bread to feed our bodies. He wants our stubbornness broken into humble obedience.

Vance Havner

Jesus is Victor. Calvary is the place of victory. Obedience is the pathway of victory. Bible study and prayer is the preparation for victory.

Corrie ten Boom

Therefore, get your minds ready for action, being self-disciplined, and set your hope completely on the grace to be brought to you at the revelation of Jesus Christ. As obedient children, do not be conformed to the desires of your former ignorance but, as the One who called you is holy, you also are to be holy in all your conduct.

1 Peter 1:13-15 Holman CSB

And the world with its lust is passing away, but the one who does God's will remains forever.

1 John 2:17 Holman CSB

A PRAYER

Dear Heavenly Father, You have blessed me with a love that is infinite and eternal. Let me demonstrate my love for You by obeying Your commandments. Make me a faithful servant, Father, today and throughout eternity. And, let me show my love for You by sharing Your message and Your love with others. Amen

Chapter 22

Christ Matters Because...

HE GIVES YOU THE POWER TO ACCOMPLISH MIRACULOUS THINGS

I assure you: If anyone says to this mountain,
"Be lifted up and thrown into the sea,"
and does not doubt in his heart,
but believes that what he says will happen,
it will be done for him.

—

Mark 11:23 Holman CSB

The author of Hebrews makes the point clearly and forcefully: the just shall live by faith. When a suffering woman sought healing by merely touching the hem of His cloak, Jesus replied, "Daughter, be of good comfort; thy faith hath made thee whole" (Matthew 9:22 KJV). The message to believers of every generation is clear: live by faith today and every day. But, when we face adversity, illness, or heartbreak, living by faith can be difficult indeed.

Concentration camp survivor Corrie ten Boom relied on faith during her ten months of imprisonment and torture. Later, despite the fact that four of her family members had died in Nazi death camps, Corrie's faith was unshaken. She wrote, "There is no pit so deep that God's love is not deeper still." Christians take note: Genuine faith in God means faith in all circumstances, happy or sad, joyful or tragic. If your faith is being tested to the point of breaking, know that your Savior is near. If you reach out to Him in faith, He will give you peace and heal your broken spirit. Be content to touch even the smallest fragment of the Master's garment, and He will make you whole.

There are a lot of things in life that are difficult to understand. Faith allows the soul to go beyond what the eyes can see.

John Maxwell

The popular idea of faith is of a certain obstinate optimism: the hope, tenaciously held in the face of trouble, that the universe is fundamentally friendly and things may get better.

J. I. Packer

Faith is seeing light with the eyes of your heart, when the eyes of your body see only darkness.

Barbara Johnson

Just as our faith strengthens our prayer life, so do our prayers deepen our faith. Let us pray often, starting today, for a deeper, more powerful faith.

Shirley Dobson

I am truly grateful that faith enables me to move past the question of "Why?"

Zig Ziglar

I am able to do all things through Him who strengthens me.

Philippians 4:13 Holman CSB

Now faith is the reality of what is hoped for, the proof of what is not seen.

Hebrews 11:1 Holman CSB

For we walk by faith, not by sight.

2 Corinthians 5:7 Holman CSB

A PRAYER

Dear Lord, I want faith that moves mountains. You have big plans for this world and big plans for me. Help me fulfill those plans, Father, as I follow in the footsteps of Your Son. Amen

Chapter 23

Christ Matters Because...

HE SHOWS YOU
THE IMPORTANCE
OF PRAYER

Very early in the morning,
while it was still dark, He got up, went out,
and made His way to a deserted place.
And He was praying there.

—

Mark 1:35 Holman CSB

Are you a prayer warrior, or have you retreated from God's battlefield? Do you pray about almost everything or about almost nothing? Do you pray only at mealtimes, or do you pray at all times? The answer to these questions will determine, to a surprising extent, the degree to which God will use you for the glory of His kingdom.

Jesus made it clear to His disciples: they should pray always. And so should we. Genuine, heartfelt prayer changes things and it changes us. When we lift our hearts to our Father in heaven, we open ourselves to a never-ending source of divine wisdom and infinite love.

Your prayers are powerful, so pray. And as you go about your daily activities, remember God's instructions: "Rejoice always! Pray constantly. Give thanks in everything, for this is God's will for you in Christ Jesus" (1 Thessalonians 5:16-18 Holman CSB). Start praying in the morning and keep praying until you fall off to sleep at night. And rest assured: God is always listening, and He always wants to hear from you.

We must leave it to God to answer our prayers in His own wisest way. Sometimes, we are so impatient and think that God does not answer. God always answers! He never fails! Be still. Abide in Him.

Mrs. Charles E. Cowman

When you ask God to do something, don't ask timidly; put your whole heart into it.

Marie T. Freeman

God delights in the prayers of His children— prayers that express our love for Him, prayers that share our deepest burdens with Him.

Billy Graham

Are you weak? Weary? Confused? Troubled? Pressured? How is your relationship with God? Is it held in its place of priority? I believe the greater the pressure, the greater your need for time alone with Him.

Kay Arthur

The Christian on his knees sees more than the philosopher on tiptoe.

D. L. Moody

The intense prayer of the righteous is very powerful.

James 5:16 Holman CSB

Let the words of my mouth and the meditation of my heart be acceptable in Your sight, O Lord, my strength and my Redeemer.

Psalm 19:14 NKJV

Yet He often withdrew to deserted places and prayed.

Luke 5:16 Holman CSB

A PRAYER

Dear Lord, let me raise my hopes and my dreams, my worries and my fears to You. Let me be a worthy example to family and friends, showing them the importance and the power of prayer. Let me take everything to You in prayer, Lord, and when I do, let me trust in Your answers. Amen

Chapter 24

Christ Matters Because...

YOU MUST STRIVE TO PLEASE HIM FIRST

For am I now trying to win the favor of people,
or God? Or am I striving to please people?
If I were still trying to please people,
I would not be a slave of Christ.

—

Galatians 1:10 Holman CSB

As you seek to discover God's purpose for your life, you will inevitably confront the expectations and demands of life here on earth. Perhaps the pressures of caring for your family or the stresses of building your career have placed a heavy weight upon your shoulders. Whatever your circumstances, remember this: your first responsibility is to trust God and to obey His commandments. Obedience to Him is determined, not by words, but by deeds. Talking about righteousness is easy; living righteously and responsibly is far more difficult, especially in today's temptation-filled world.

When Jesus was tempted by Satan, the Master's response was unambiguous. Jesus chose to worship the Lord and serve Him only. We, as followers of Christ, must follow in His footsteps. When we place God in a position of secondary importance, we do ourselves great harm. But, when we imitate Jesus and place the Lord in His rightful place—at the center of our lives—then we claim spiritual treasures that will endure forever.

Who will you try to please today: God or man? Your primary obligation is not to please imperfect men and women. Your obligation is to strive diligently to meet the expectations of an all-knowing and perfect God. Trust Him always. Love Him always. Praise Him always. And seek to please Him. Always.

Fashion is an enduring testimony to the fact that we live quite consciously before the eyes of others.

John Eldredge

Never be afraid of the world's censure; it's praise is much more to be dreaded.

C. H. Spurgeon

Too many Christians have geared their program to please, to entertain, and to gain favor from this world. We are concerned with how much, instead of how little, like this age we can become.

Billy Graham

He who walks with wise men will be wise, but the companion of fools will be destroyed.

Proverbs 13:20 NKJV

For am I now trying to win the favor of people, or God? Or am I striving to please people? If I were still trying to please people, I would not be a slave of Christ.

Galatians 1:10 Holman CSB

Stay away from a foolish man; you will gain no knowledge from his speech.

Proverbs 14:7 Holman CSB

A PRAYER

Dear Lord, today I will worry less about pleasing other people and more about pleasing You. I will honor You with my thoughts, my actions, and my prayers. And I will worship You, Father, with thanksgiving in my heart, this day and forever. Amen

Chapter 25

Christ Matters Because...

HIS ATTITUDE
SHOWS YOU
HOW TO LIVE

Make your own attitude that of Christ Jesus.

—

Philippians 2:5 Holman CSB

The Christian life is a cause for celebration, but sometimes we don't feel much like celebrating. In fact, when the weight of the world seems to bear down upon our shoulders, celebration may be the last thing on our minds . . . but it shouldn't be. As God's children, we are all blessed beyond measure on good days and bad. This day is a non-renewable resource— once it's gone, it's gone forever. We should give thanks for this day while using it for the glory of God.

What will your attitude be today? Will you be fearful, angry, bored, or worried? Will you be cynical, bitter or pessimistic? If so, God wants to have a little talk with you.

God created you in His own image, and He wants you to experience joy and abundance. But, God will not force His joy upon you; you must claim it for yourself. So today, and every day hereafter, celebrate the life that God has given you. Think optimistically about yourself and your future. Give thanks to the One who has given you everything, and trust in your heart that He wants to give you so much more.

A positive attitude will have positive results
because attitudes are contagious.

Zig Ziglar

The people whom I have seen succeed best
in life have always been cheerful and hopeful
people who went about their business with a
smile on their faces.

Charles Kingsley

If you can't tell whether your glass is half-empty
of half-full, you don't need another glass; what
you need is better eyesight . . . and a more
thankful heart.

Marie T. Freeman

Life is 10% what happens to you and 90% how
you respond to it.

Charles Swindoll

Life goes on. Keep on smiling and the whole
world smiles with you.

Dennis Swanberg

Set your minds on what is above, not on what is on the earth.

Colossians 3:2 Holman CSB

For the word of God is living and powerful, and sharper than any two-edged sword, piercing even to the division of soul and spirit, and of joints and marrow, and is a discerner of the thoughts and intents of the heart.

Hebrews 4:12 NKJV

A PRAYER

Lord, I pray for an attitude that is Christlike. Whatever my circumstances, whether good or bad, triumphal or tragic, let my response reflect a God-honoring attitude of optimism, faith, and love for You. Amen

Chapter 26

Christ Matters Because . . .

HE DESERVES
YOUR PRAISE

*Therefore, through Him let us continually offer
up to God a sacrifice of praise, that is,
the fruit of our lips that confess His name.*

—

Hebrews 13:15 Holman CSB

Because we have been saved by God's only Son, we must never lose hope in the priceless gifts of eternal love and eternal life. And, because we are so richly blessed, we must approach our Heavenly Father with reverence and thanksgiving.

Sometimes, in our rush "to get things done," we simply don't stop long enough to pause and thank our Creator for the countless blessings He has bestowed upon us. But when we slow down and express our gratitude to the One who made us, we enrich our own lives and the lives of those around us.

Thanksgiving should become a habit, a regular part of our daily routines. God has blessed us beyond measure, and we owe Him everything, including our eternal praise. Let us praise Him today, tomorrow, and throughout eternity.

Praise and thank God for who He is and for what He has done for you.

Billy Graham

The joy of the Holy Spirit is experienced by giving thanks in all situations.

Bill Bright

It is always possible to be thankful for what is given rather than to complain about what is not given. One or the other becomes a habit of life.

Elisabeth Elliot

The act of thanksgiving is a demonstration of the fact that you are going to trust and believe God.

Kay Arthur

God is worthy of our praise and is pleased when we come before Him with thanksgiving.

Shirley Dobson

Enter into His gates with thanksgiving, and into His courts with praise. Be thankful to Him, and bless His name. For the Lord is good; His mercy is everlasting, and His truth endures to all generations.

Psalm 100:4-5 NKJV

So that at the name of Jesus every knee should bow—of those who are in heaven and on earth and under the earth—and every tongue should confess that Jesus Christ is Lord, to the glory of God the Father.

Philippians 2:10-11 Holman CSB

A PRAYER

Heavenly Father, I come to You today with hope in my heart and praise on my lips. I place my trust in You, Dear Lord, knowing that with You as my Protector, I have nothing to fear. I thank You, Lord, for Your grace, for Your love, and for Your Son. Let me follow in Christ's footsteps today and every day that I live. And then, when my work here is done, let me live with You forever. Amen

Chapter 27

Christ Matters Because...

IN HIS CHURCH, YOU WILL FIND FELLOWSHIP

Now I urge you, brothers, in the name of our Lord Jesus Christ, that you all say the same thing, that there be no divisions among you, and that you be united with the same understanding and the same conviction.

—

1 Corinthians 1:10 Holman CSB

Fellowship with other believers should be an integral part of your everyday life. Your association with fellow Christians should be uplifting, enlightening, encouraging, and consistent.

Are you an active member of your own fellowship? Are you a builder of bridges inside the four walls of your church and outside it? Do you contribute to God's glory by contributing your time and your talents to a close-knit band of believers? Hopefully so. The fellowship of believers is intended to be a powerful tool for spreading God's Good News and uplifting His children. And God intends for you to be a fully contributing member of that fellowship. Your intentions should be the same.

One of the ways God refills us after failure is through the blessing of Christian fellowship. Just experiencing the joy of simple activities shared with other children of God can have a healing effect on us.

Anne Graham Lotz

And if our fellowship below in Jesus be so sweet, what greater blessings shall we know when round His throne we meet?

Charles Wesley

Be united with other Christians. A wall with loose bricks is not good. The bricks must be cemented together.

Corrie ten Boom

If you dine alone, you miss the best part of the meal: the fellowship.

Dennis Swanberg

*The one who loves his brother remains in the light,
and there is no cause for stumbling in him.*

1 John 2:10 Holman CSB

*Now finally, all of you should be like-minded
and sympathetic, should love believers, and be
compassionate and humble.*

1 Peter 3:8 Holman CSB

*Therefore, as we have opportunity, we must work
for the good of all, especially for those who belong to
the household of faith.*

Galatians 6:10 Holman CSB

A PRAYER

Heavenly Father, You have given me a
community of supporters called the church. Let
our fellowship be a reflection of the love we
feel for each other and the love we feel for You.
Amen

Chapter 28

Christ Matters Because...

THROUGH HIM YOU CAN CELEBRATE LIFE

Rejoice in the Lord always.
I will say it again: Rejoice!

—

Philippians 4:4 Holman CSB

Are you living a life of agitation, consternation, or celebration? If you're a believer, it should most certainly be the latter. With Christ as your Savior, every day should be a time of celebration.

Oswald Chambers correctly observed, "Joy is the great note all throughout the Bible." C. S. Lewis echoed that thought when he wrote, "Joy is the serious business of heaven." But, even the most dedicated Christians can, on occasion, forget to celebrate each day for what it is: a priceless gift from God.

Today, celebrate the life that God has given you. Today, put a smile on your face, kind words on your lips, and a song in your heart. Be generous with your praise and free with your encouragement. And then, when you have celebrated life to the fullest, invite your friends to do likewise. After all, this is God's day, and He has given us clear instructions for its use. We are commanded to rejoice and be glad. So, with no further ado, let the celebration begin . . .

If you can forgive the person you were, accept the person you are, and believe in the person you will become, you are headed for joy. So celebrate your life.

Barbara Johnson

Some of us seem so anxious about avoiding hell that we forget to celebrate our journey toward heaven.

Philip Yancey

Joy is the keynote of the Christian life. It is not something that happens. It is a gift, given to us in the coming of Christ.

Elisabeth Elliot

Each day, each moment is so pregnant with eternity that if we "tune in" to it, we can hardly contain the joy.

Gloria Gaither

As Catherine of Siena said, "All the way to heaven is heaven." A joyful end requires a joyful means. Bless the Lord.

Eugene Peterson

David and the whole house of Israel were celebrating before the Lord.

2 Samuel 6:5 Holman CSB

Their sorrow was turned into rejoicing and their mourning into a holiday. They were to be days of feasting, rejoicing, and of sending gifts to one another and the poor.

Esther 9:22 Holman CSB

At the dedication of the wall of Jerusalem, they sent for the Levites wherever they lived and brought them to Jerusalem to celebrate the joyous dedication with thanksgiving and singing accompanied by cymbals, harps, and lyres.

Nehemiah 12:27 Holman CSB

A PRAYER

Dear Lord, let me celebrate this moment and every moment of life. Let me celebrate You and Your marvelous creation, Father, and let me give thanks for this day. Today is Your gift to me, Lord. Let me use it to Your glory while giving all the praise to You. Amen

Chapter 29

Christ Matters Because...

HE GIVES YOUR LIFE MEANING

For we are His making, created in Christ Jesus for good works, which God prepared ahead of time so that we should walk in them.

—

Ephesians 2:10 Holman CSB

God has a plan for your life—a plan that is near and dear to His heart. If you genuinely seek to fulfill God's plan for your life, then you must do this: you must make decisions that are pleasing to Him. The most important decision of your life is, of course, your commitment to accept God's Son as your personal Lord and Savior. And, once your eternal destiny is secured, you will undoubtedly ask yourself the question "What now, Lord?" If you earnestly seek God's will, you will find it . . . in time.

Life is best lived on purpose. And purpose, like everything else in the universe, begins in the heart of God. Whether you realize it or not, God has a direction for your life, a divine calling, a path along which He intends to lead you. When you welcome God into your heart and establish a genuine relationship with Him, He will begin—and He will continue—to make His purposes known.

Sometimes, God's intentions will be clear to you; other times, God's plan will seem uncertain at best. But even on those difficult days when you are unsure which way to turn, you must never lose sight of these overriding facts: God created you for a reason; He has important work for you to do; and He's waiting patiently for you to do it. So why not begin today?

God is more concerned with the direction of your life than with its speed.

Marie T. Freeman

Oh Lord, let me not live to be useless.

John Wesley

Without God, life has no purpose, and without purpose, life has no meaning.

Rick Warren

Whatever purpose motivates your life, it must be something big enough and grand enough to make the investment worthwhile.

Warren Wiersbe

For it is God who is working among you both the willing and the working for His good purpose.

Philippians 2:13 Holman CSB

We know that all things work together for the good of those who love God: those who are called according to His purpose.

Romans 8:28 Holman CSB

I will instruct you and show you the way to go; with My eye on you, I will give counsel.

Psalm 32:8 Holman CSB

A PRAYER

Dear Lord, we seek to live meaningful lives; we will turn to You to find that meaning. We will study Your Word, we will obey Your commandments, we will trust Your providence, and we will honor Your Son. Give us Your blessings, Father, and lead our family along a path that is pleasing to You, today, tomorrow, and forever. Amen

Chapter 30

Christ Matters Because...

HE GIVES YOU PEACE

Peace I leave with you. My peace I give to you.
I do not give to you as the world gives.
Your heart must not be troubled or fearful.

—

John 14:27 Holman CSB

Oftentimes, our outer struggles are simply manifestations of the inner conflict that we feel when we stray from God's path.

Have you found the genuine peace that can be yours through Jesus Christ? Or are you still rushing after the illusion of "peace and happiness" that the world promises but cannot deliver? The beautiful words of John 14:27 remind us that Jesus offers us peace, not as the world gives, but as He alone gives: "Peace I leave with you. My peace I give to you. I do not give to you as the world gives. Your heart must not be troubled or fearful." Our challenge is to accept Christ's peace into our hearts and then, as best we can, to share His peace with our neighbors.

Today, as a gift to yourself, to your family, and to your friends, claim the inner peace that is your spiritual birthright: the peace of Jesus Christ. It is offered freely; it has been paid for in full; it is yours for the asking. So ask. And then share.

He wants us to have a faith that does not complain while waiting, but rejoices because we know our times are in His hands—nail-scarred hands that labor for our highest good.

Kay Arthur

A life of intimacy with God is characterized by joy.

Oswald Chambers

Lord, I thank you for the promise of heaven and the unexpected moments when you touch my heartstrings with that longing for my eternal home.

Joni Eareckson Tada

God knows everything. He can manage everything, and He loves us. Surely this is enough for a fullness of joy that is beyond words.

Hannah Whitall Smith

God gives to us a heavenly gift called joy, radically different in quality from any natural joy.

Elisabeth Elliot

God has called us to peace.

1 Corinthians 7:15 NKJV

Be of good comfort, be of one mind, live in peace; and the God of love and peace will be with you.

2 Corinthians 13:11 NKJV

For He is our peace.

Ephesians 2:14 Holman CSB

A PRAYER

Dear Lord, the peace that the world offers is fleeting, but You offer a peace that is perfect and eternal. Let me take my concerns and burdens to You, Father, and let me feel the spiritual abundance that You offer through the person of Your Son, the Prince of Peace. Amen